POOLE
PAST & PRESENT

IAN ANDREWS & FRANK HENSON

The
History
Press

First published 2009

The History Press
The Mill, Brimscombe Port
Stroud, Gloucestershire, GL5 2QG
www.thehistorypress.co.uk

British Library Cataloguing in Publication Data.
A catalogue record for this book is available from the British Library.

ISBN 978 0 7524 5286 9

Printed in Great Britain

CONTENTS

Acknowledgements   4

Introduction   5

1   Hamworthy and Poole Quay   7

2   High Street and Old Town   19

3   From Poole Park to Lower Parkstone   31

4   Lilliput to County Gates   43

5   Branksome, Upper Parkstone and Newtown   61

6   Longfleet to Northern Poole   79

ACKNOWLEDGEMENTS

The authors have gathered the material in this book from their own collections and acknowledge the help and permission they have received from many good friends who are the owners of postcards and their own cherished family pictures, some of which they have been unable to include in the 'final cut':

E. Ballance
Birchmere Ltd
P. Broad
S. Burns
W. Carter
R. Clark
R. Farley
B. Fenwick
G. Frend
B.J. Galpin
R. Gosling
The late J. Grebby
D. Griffiths
Hall & Woodhouse Ltd
J. Hart
A. Hawkes
D. Haxall
The late T. Hearl
Lord Iliffe
The late I.M. Hoare
M. Legg
B. Leverett

R. Lines
E. Moore
I. Morris
The late D. Orchard
M. Phillipson
Poole Historical Trust
Poole Museum and Local History Centre
Poole Town FC Supporters' Club
Ryvita Company Ltd
The late N. Skinner
A. Smeaton
The late D. Smith
F. Smith
The late S. Swain
H. Thorby
N. Tolson
M. Tombs
P. Toms
J. Trim
P. Wilnecker
A. Yeatman
K. Young

Every effort has been made to obtain permission from copyright owners, and the authors apologise if any have been omitted or overlooked.

INTRODUCTION

Poole has a long history and only a fraction of it has taken place since photography was invented. Inevitably, a book such as this can therefore only be an impression of the many facets of the town.

Poole is many different things to different people, and the authors have attempted to reflect this. Probably the longest traditions are those emanating from the harbour, such as the shipping, fishing and the trades and skills that supported them, and the changes in the Quay from a working area bustling with ships and warehouses (and a railway line) to a tourist and pleasure craft haven. But the pubs have survived this change.

Turning to the beaches, it was not until the Council made efforts to encourage tourism in the 1930s that this emphasis made an impact on the beach scene, as following photographs show.

There was an explosion of people and businesses from the 1960s onwards and many new inhabitants and their families knew little of the old High Street shops, or the run-down, overcrowded houses with inadequate living facilities, let alone access through narrow streets, courtyards and alleyways unsuited for the age of universal car ownership that lay behind them. They would be surprised to see what a difference the indoor air-conditioned Dolphin Centre has made.

The town has sacrificed heathlands to invest in modern housing and factories, needed to stem the decline of the economy after the Second World War. New high-tech and office employments have arisen to give well-educated, local young people a chance to make a living in their birthplace, alongside incoming labour.

In some cases, there is very little physical difference in the appearance of the streets, but in shopping areas we have illustrated the decline of the corner shops and the rise of the cafés, restaurants, clubs, charity shops and estate agents occupying the same buildings, or in the case of supermarkets, the move to the outskirts.

In the case of pubs, Poole currently has a plentiful supply, and it may seem surprising that there were once even more!

There are records of occupations that are now a thing of the past, and of traditional skills, such as clayworking, that have taken the town's name round the world but which are currently precariously poised. Other firms have now established themselves and today take Poole's name far and wide, such as Ryvita, Sunseeker and Lush.

Although not technically in Poole, the presence of Brownsea Island and its ownership by the National Trust has opened up the town to many visitors who have to pass through the town to reach the island and the birthplace of the worldwide Scouting movement.

The manufacturing industry and demands for manual labour have been replaced by service and health industries, giving rise to more job opportunities for women, part-time and flexitime working. Not a lot of people appreciate the number of HQ buildings scattered round the town – for example, Merlin Entertainments and Animal, as well as a modern presence for Barclays.

Speedway in Poole Stadium remains the town's foremost professional sport and maintains a leading position, winning many trophies in recent years. Greyhound racing also draws audiences from a wide radius and shares the stadium originally built for football. Unlike northern towns, soccer has never progressed beyond non-league status, but this disguises the enthusiasm existing for the sport. In the harbour, the status of the yacht clubs and their races remains at a high level – Poole Week still follows Cowes. Parkstone and Broadstone golf courses are the oldest in the town, joined later by Knighton Heath and more recently Canford Magna. Indoor sporting facilities for swimming, squash, badminton and bowls, together with health clubs, are all relatively modern additions. Over the years Poole has had a fair share of national and Olympic contestants, for example Percy Baker in bowls, Bill Harvell in cycling, Betty Uber in badminton and Rodney Pattisson, who won gold in the 1968 and 1972 Olympics for sailing.

For eight years, Poole had the role of being the UK's only international airport. From 1938, throughout the war, BOAC flying boats maintained civilian air links on long distance horseshoe routes to Asia, Africa and the Americas, and both the RAF and Fleet Air Arm had military flying boat/seaplane bases in the harbour.

The arrival of the iron road in Hamworthy (Poole's first railway station) in 1847 was part of an intended international route, being followed in 1849 by the inauguration of a steamship to the Channel Isles. An attempt to create a regular ferry to Cherbourg in 1865 was short-lived, unlike the present daily freight and passenger sailings from the port, inaugurated in 1973. Until 1872 there was no direct rail link through Bournemouth to and from London, and passengers would travel via Wimborne and Ringwood to Lymington on 'Castleman's Corkscrew'.

The Council's foresight for the need for cheap and easy communication with Bournemouth for workers led to the establishment of a tram service through to Christchurch in 1901. In 1935 trams gave way to buses. A little-known fact is that there has been a bus service from County Gates to the Haven since 1905 – the oldest surviving unaltered bus route in the UK.

The oldest dual carriageway in the country is at Upton Road, created by a pioneering Borough Engineer, Ernest Goodacre, who also had a vision (fast disappearing as roads are widened and 'improved') that all the approach roads to the town should be tree-lined avenues, the best surviving example being at Gravel Hill. Yet still Poole has a feature that dates back to the days of horse and cart – the railway crossing (now for pedestrians only) that interrupts High Street.

The pre-war period saw a rash of new secondary school plans coming to fruition and giving rise to new developments replacing longstanding schools, including the Boys' and Girls' Grammar Schools.

The growth of Bournemouth and its suburbs from the 1860s owes a great deal to Poole supplying the building and road-making materials and skills. It was a matter of controversy when the Bournemouth Symphony Orchestra and the university moved their bases to Poole that the name Bournemouth was retained. And now, with the addition of the new Bournemouth Arts University College, Poole has two geographically misnamed universities! But then it has, in its own right, produced two 'Miss Worlds'.

1

HAMWORTHY AND POOLE QUAY

Poole Power Station, 1950.

The Point at Rockley, *c.* 1958. Part of the Rockley estate at Ham Common was used as HMS *Turtle* during the Second World War. After the war, the Council decided that in order to promote Poole as a tourist centre, a holiday park should be allowed on part of the common. The holiday park, Rockley Sands Ltd, was opened in1957 by Messrs Levy and Stone after the Council had purchased Lord Rockley's estate (with the exception of the old clay pit lake, required by the Royal Marine base for training purposes). The first facilities manager at the camp was Reg Still, who was promoted to general manager in 1960. At various times in its history the complex has had a petrol station, amusement arcade and a miniature train. The Palladium Ballroom was opened in 1966, and among the many stars that appeared there was television comedian Freddie Frinton. A sailing school was established at the lower end of the area and a public access road through the camp to the common was maintained.

The farmhouse in Lake Road, Hamworthy, was already long established when this picture was taken at the turn of the twentieth century. When the farmhouse was built this part of Hamworthy was predominately agricultural land. In around 1770 it had ten acres attached. It was let to James Stephen (ancestor of Virginia Woolf) as a base for him as manager for Sir John Webb of Canford's planned maritime village, with a clay and even coal mining and boatbuilding business, 'as there was no estate suitable for a gentleman's residence nearby.' James Stephen's son wrote that the area was 'plagued by gnats.' The house has seen little alteration since the original picture was taken, but the farmland has been sold off over the years for residential development. There are also extensive old clay workings in this area.

Hamworthy has always played an important role in building and maintaining ships, especially in the days of canvas and sail. One of the essentials was rope, used for sheets, nets and fishing and, of course, for securing anchors. Today the Municipal and Owen Carter Almshouses in Blandford Road stand on the site of one of the old ropewalks. Displaying a rope used for a prize tug-of-war are women typically dressed in their work clothes, whose task was literally to walk the strands from a post, twisting them as they went.

The Hamworthy Bridge, *c.* 1932. The channel between the Quay and Hamworthy was first bridged by a wooden construction in 1834, at a cost of £9,600 met by the Lord of the Manor of Canford and local Member of Parliament, W.F.S. Ponsonby. Ponsonby, a Liberal, promoted a private Parliamentary Bill to get permission to build the bridge to the annoyance of the Conservative-controlled Council. This was replaced in 1885 by an iron swing bridge to allow larger ships access to the wharves at West Quay. A toll of 1*d* was levied for crossing the bridge. The Council bought the bridge in 1926 for £16,000 and promptly abolished the toll. The present lifting bridge was constructed by the Cleveland Bridge Company (recently involved in building the new Wembley Stadium) at a cost of £60,000 and opened in 1927. This 1930s photograph shows an Anglo American Oil Company petrol tanker after leaving the company's wharf at West Quay.

The Victoria Mill of W.H. Yeatman & Sons dates back to a merchant mariner, Thomas Young, in the early 1700s. The mill went through several changes of ownership before William Yeatman leased the buildings in 1880. The present frontage was added in 1881. W.H. Yeatman & Sons was founded at Wareham in around 1867. Their move to Poole in 1880 saw expansion of the business, which was fully concentrated on the site after a fire destroyed the Canford Mill in 1894. The company bought surrounding premises to enlarge the production facilities. In June 1942, a delayed-action fire bomb destroyed the milling equipment and most of the production was suspended until after the war, when the mill was refurbished with more modern machinery. The firm continued in the manufacture of animal foodstuffs until October 1974. After the closing of the mill the building was converted to restaurants and flats. The lorry driver in the 1960s photograph is Phil Faletto, whilst Bert Elmes, a long-time employee, looks on.

Local recruits, having taken up the appeal for 'King and Country', proudly march off to war along the Quay, past the Custom House, watched by apprehensive friends and relatives. The Union flag flies over the then Harbour Office. In modern times the eighteenth-century Custom House has become a restaurant and HM Coastguard occupy the old Harbour Office, now that the centre of commercial maritime activity has transferred to Hamworthy.

Belben's Flour Mill on the Quay was one of many firms that dominated the waterfront. The mill burnt down during the Second World War and the site was acquired by Christopher Hill Ltd, a firm of agriculture merchants, for their head offices. Christopher Hill was absorbed into the Rank Hovis MacDougall group in 1960, and later by Dalgety's. The Harbour Commissioners moved into the offices in the 1970s. After it was vacated in the early 1990s when the commissioners moved to Hamworthy, the office building was demolished. The character of the Quay altered as the tourist and leisure industry became important to the local economy. A bar was built on the site, with accommodation on the upper floors.

The broad swathe of Poole Quay, bustling with railway wagons, horses and carts and cargo boats in 1920, now supports a lively leisure industry as former warehouses have found new uses, mainly as (yet more) pubs, cafés and places of entertainment. In summertime, Tuesday night has become known for miles around for its gathering of motorbikes by the thousand, while firework displays on Thursdays and gatherings of classic cars on Fridays bring in the summer crowds.

In the distance, the pottery that took the name of Poole all over the world has succumbed to apartments above factory outlets, in an architectural style sadly not reflecting local heritage or indigenous materials. More profit can now be made this way than by producing tea sets and decorated pots.

Poole Pottery stood on the Quay for over 100 years, employing many local people and took the name of Poole around the globe. The factory kilns on the site produced tableware and decorative pieces to the highest standards of contemporary design. Mrs Doris Young, whose job was to apply the distinctive dolphin backstamps, is pictured with cups stacked ready for firing.

The 1990s brought difficult times as corporate owners valued the business more for its site value than pottery profits. It was controversially redeveloped, and the pottery business was ultimately bought from administrators by a firm which transferred the tableware production to Staffordshire, retaining only a showroom presence and a small design studio in Poole.

The East Quay, *c.* 1930. When the depth of the water at the Quay became a problem in the 1890s, as it was insufficient for larger ships to use the wharf, the Quay was extended eastwards towards deeper water. This was important for the colliers delivering coal to the gasworks, as seen in the background of the picture. The coal was unloaded by the large overhead grabs and transported very dustily to the main gas-making plant by overhead cableways across the lower town. With the introduction of North Sea gas, the gas-making plant was closed in 1968 and the overhead gantries were dismantled.

Today a yacht haven adjoins the Quay. It took away quayside space for cars to park and have an undisturbed view down the harbour, to the regret of many, but presents a much cleaner face.

The Fishermens' Dock, *c.* 1959. The Fishermens' Dock was a protective wall built off the eastern end of the Quay as an offshore mooring area for the local fishing boats. It had easy access to the East Quay wall where the small tenders for the larger fishing fleet could be tied up. The fishing boat owners constructed wooden frames on the ground behind the Quay wall to dry and repair their nets. In the background of the picture are Baiter and Whitecliff before the infill development for Baiter Park. The dock area was enlarged to accommodate more and larger boats and to meet stringent new EU regulations when the yacht haven, now owned entirely by the Harbour Commissioners, was built off the Quay.

2

HIGH STREET AND OLD TOWN

New Orchard, *c.* 1908.

In the nineteenth century the town's first library was established by a gift from the town's MPs as Poole Literary Institute, in a prominent position at the bottom of High Street. After the establishment of a public circulating library by the Council, it became the Cornelia Working Mens' Club and later the Missions to Seamen. After the Second World War it was Young Citizens House, a youth club. It was then redeveloped as the HQ of Poole Harbour Commissioners. When they moved out to the former Christopher Hill offices on the Quay (later moving again to Hamworthy) it became the offices and entrance to the Waterfront Museum.

In 2007 a major National Lottery award enabled the Council to completely remodel and rename it as Poole Museum, incorporating a striking glass and steel entrance designed by the prizewinning international architect, Richard Horden.

In 1923 storms blew down the brick frontage of Scaplen's Court in High Street, which more than twenty years earlier had been divided into at least eight tenements with over thirty occupants, and revealed a much older stone building. Its importance was soon recognized. The newly-formed Society of Poole Men stepped in to purchase this ancient monument, opening it as a museum, as the Council displayed no interest until 1931 when it finally agreed to buy it. For many years it was open to the public under the name of 'The Old Town House'. Prominent in the foreground is a police call box, for use in emergencies.

Today's photograph shows Scaplen's Court Museum, roofed and restored to its original height in the original style with English Heritage blessing in 1986. Nowadays the use of the museum is restricted to school parties, with the Poole Men being allowed to hold one Open Day a year. The pole on the left is the modern equivalent of the police box, as it directs CCTV cameras observing High Street.

W.J. Bacon's ironmonger's shop (later Bacon & Curtis Ltd) succeeded a similar business established by G.S. Norton in an area of High Street that was known as the Square or Cornmarket, This was used as a vegetable marketplace, and is now fenced off and used as forecourts under licence from the highway authority. In the 1970s redevelopment of the premises for office use by Barclays as Latimer House took place. Today a television and hi-fi shop occupies the ground floor. On the left are premises formerly occupied by a local bank, Poole Town & County Bank, and later the Wilts & Dorset Bank. In turn this became National Provincial (now NatWest). It is now used as Alcatraz, an Italian restaurant. On the right-hand side of the Square, a Sainsbury's local store has been opened beneath former offices, now converted to Orchard Plaza.

Old Orchard lies between Lagland Street and High Street. On the corner was Albert Satelle's tobacconists, with another shop at No. 119a High Street. The workshop advertised by H.J. Cole & Sons, house furnishers and undertakers, was in Kendall's Alley, which ran from Lagland Street to High Street. The single-storey brick building on the left of the old picture was a rather smelly public toilet!

A public car park was at the rear of the toilets and was replaced by a multi-storey block now called the Quay Visitors' Car Park. The road was widened in the early 1970s when the traffic flow of the lower town and High Street was re-routed.

In the background of the modern view are some of the flats that were built when the houses in the east of the Old Town were demolished. Behind hoardings on the right, a former Inland Revenue office is being converted to apartments with a Sainsbury's supermarket at ground floor level.

Skinner Street United Reformed Church was built in 1777 and the old chapel on the site, built in 1760 at a cost of £374 7s 7d, became an institute and later a school. It dominated the lower part of Lagland Street. Skinner Street Sunday School was the first in the town – the earliest known reference to it was in 1787. The building was also used as a day school, later as the British School, on weekdays. The education was very basic, and children had to pay a fee of a penny or tuppence a week towards the cost. The original building had to be enlarged in 1833. Despite struggling at times, it continued as a school until the opening of South Road School in 1912.

The large hall of the building was modernised and continues to be used by various organisations, but the school frontage was demolished in the 1980s. This railed-off area has opened up fine views of the listed Skinner Street (UR) Church building.

The next-door New London Inn has been renamed 'the Cockleshell' to commemorate the role played in the Second World War by Special Forces established and trained in the town.

Looking towards High Street from Dear Hay Lane in 1974, the premises, then occupied by
Weston's DIY, were originally part of Styring's Poole Brewery.

In the 1930s it was occupied by Mundell & Bollam, grocery wholesalers and suppliers.
A large copper vat, left by the brewery when it closed, was used by Mundell & Bollam to
boil hams that were then smoked in an old brewery oast house. Mundell & Bollam became
part of the Misselbrook & Weston group which transferred to Waterloo Road. Harry
Weston, popularly known as 'Hardboard Harry', then opened a DIY business here until it
was demolished to build an indoor market. This venture was not a great success and after
it closed alterations were made to allow it to become Poole's Jobcentre Plus.

The White Horse Inn at West Quay Road was the last of four public houses to survive in the road. The others were the Bridge Inn, the White Hart and the Wheatsheaf. The latter closed in the 1930s and the demolition of residential properties in this area meant a loss of trade and the eventual closure of the other pubs.

Sunseeker International is a renowned maker of luxury motor yachts with a global market, and is now the major employer in Poole with other premises along West Quay Road and New Quay Road, Hamworthy, and a development unit at Tower Park, as well as interests at Portland Harbour.

B. Shutler's boatyard in West Quay Road (pictured around 1930) was on the west shore, fronting Holes Bay. The workmen in the picture are overhauling the lifeboat *Harmar* that served Poole between 1913 and 1938. Other work included speed boats for Kay Don, a regular challenger for the Harmsworth Speed Boat Trophy.

In 1943 J. Bolson & Son Ltd took over the premises and an adjoining timber yard and it played an important wartime role, building landing craft for the D-Day invasion.

After the war the former Shutler premises were sold to Christopher Hill Ltd, who installed a plant for the manufacture of cattle and poultry foodstuffs. In 1961 they built a large grain storage silo on the site. After the closure of the animal feeds mill, the site was derelict for several years until Asda purchased it for a superstore and the site for apartments and offices. The latter was earmarked for a new Barclays HQ, but after a change of their plans, they decided to stay in their present location.

Major Arthur N. Butler, CO of the Poole Home Guard, C Company ('Dads Army') is seen taking the salute outside his own furnishing shop in High Street. He was also responsible for an area known as Poole Anti-Tank Island during the war. Later, the furniture business was sold to Newbery's before becoming the Burger King franchise. Adjoining shops (an outfitters, a tobacconists, an optician and a chemist) have also had many changes of use over the years. Tydemans became Kenneth Speakes, gents' and boys' outfitters, an authorised supplier of Poole Grammar School uniforms. Oxfam now occupy this shop, with a Superdrug store nearby.

Clearly the road had been cleared of two-way traffic and buses for the parade, but today the whole of this part of High Street is pedestrianised.

Balston's Rope and Twine works in the 1870s was near the present location of Kingland Crescent and what many remember as the Ladies' Walking Field. Wrongly, this name is often assumed to be an open space dedicated to the fairer sex. In fact it was the name for a ropewalk, where the employees tediously walked between posts, making the ropes by spinning and twisting the fibres.

In 1872 the railway link to Bournemouth and Waterloo created the southern boundary of the site. Before the arcade of shops was built in Kingland Crescent, the old rope warehouse was used by White House Laundry (later relocated to Sterte).

Warn & Son were the principal motor engineers in the Old Town and their shop stood in the 1920s where Kingland Road now leads to the Bus Station and Dolphin Centre Car Park. They also had a workshop in Seldown Lane (behind the Arts Centre, now known as Lighthouse). Where can you buy good British-made tyres for your car for as little as 6s 6d (33p) or as dear as 10s (50p)? Petrol was dispensed over the pavement or bought in containers. Warn was an agent for the AA.

The last occupier of Warn's shop before this area was comprehensively redeveloped for offices and shopping was Singer Sewing Machines. Few of the local businesses formerly in the area – providing for dry cleaning, builders' supplies, bread, groceries, beer, wine and motor supplies and repair – could be incorporated in a twentieth-century indoor shopping precinct.

3

FROM POOLE PARK TO LOWER PARKSTONE

Boating in Poole Park Lake.

The Powder House at Baiter. During the late eighteenth century, Poole became a busier port, mainly through the Newfoundland trade. One of the fears of the town's leaders was that with the increase of the trade, boats carrying gunpowder might explode, causing damage and loss of life. In 1775 the Quay was extended and the stone from the old Quay was used to build the Powder House where all explosive material on board ships visiting Poole had to be stored until the ships departed. The house has been allowed to fall into ruins despite a local campaign to restore the building because of its unique history. A well-known local story is that many gardens in the Old Town had ornamental features built with stones suspiciously similar to the blocks used to build the Powder House.

White Cliff near Poole 3722

Whitecliff was not formerly as extensive an area as it is today, as the sea came up to a cliff edge that is still recognizable through gaps in the bushes of the local nature reserve.

As the earlier photograph shows, it was a popular picnic spot or resting place en route to Evening Hill and Sandbanks. During the summer, locals gathered the cockles that were abundant at low tide.

In the 1930s, the shallow tidal inlet at Whitecliff was filled with household refuse by the Council and a seaside promenade was constructed. This was extended in the 1970s to Baiter when further reclamation took place using pulverised refuse. The path alongside the harbour is extensively used by walkers and is also part of the Borough's cycle network.

While Sunday band concerts at the bandstand in Poole Park were well-known, there was much more public entertainment on high days and holidays in the past, and even impromptu performances took place. This view shows Poole Volunteers Band (later Poole Town Band) at a performance at Whitecliff in the early years of the twentieth century. Band uniforms were always smart and were changed from time to time, but the audience, even the children, were clearly not going to be outdone!

Today, children are catered for in a play area and the extensive grassed area is used for informal ball games. Whitecliff is also the designated emergency landing place for helicopters, such as the Coastguard and Air-Sea Rescue Service transferring patients to Poole Hospital and the local decompression chamber.

The playing fields and changing pavilion at Whitecliff have long been used by both senior and junior football teams and was for many years the home ground for Longfleet St Mary's FC. Two cricket wickets were also laid out for local teams.

In 1909 it was possible to look out from Whitecliff Road over a fine panoramic view of Baiter across the harbour to Branksea Island, as it was then called. Notable on Baiter were the buildings of the nineteenth-century Isolation Hospital and of the even older Powder House of 1776.

The postcard was sent with Christmas greetings at 1.15 p.m. on Christmas Eve, with no doubt by the sender that it would reach its destination by Christmas Day!

Today it is still possible to gain brief glimpses of the harbour as you drive along the road past an area designated as Whitecliff Woods. For many, this is a bonus as they drive to and from Poole Park and the shops and offices in the Old Town.

THE ZOO. POOLE PARK

Animals in the park? Well yes, there has been a long tradition from aviaries to a zoo, albeit a children's size one, started in 1963. The roar of a baby lion once housed there upset the residents, and surgery to mute it was not an option, so it was re-homed. Although it met all requirements by the authorities for the keeping of monkeys, marmosets and other small mammals that could be stroked and petted by youngsters, the public mood switched away from caged animals of any sort. Protests were mounted and eventually the zoo was run down and closed in the late 1980s.

It was therefore a delightful echo of the past when a temporary sculpture exhibition took place in 2006, featuring lifelike and life-size replicas of African animals made entirely from scrap metal materials. It attracted great interest and gave great amusement at no cost to the public.

The Sunday School Parade in 1938. Since its opening in 1890 the park has been the popular venue for many important parades and social occasions. For example, the festivities for the Silver Jubilee of King George V and the Coronation celebrations of King George VI and Queen Elizabeth II were held here. An annual Poole Hospital fundraising gala was held in the park for over forty-five years.

The older picture is of a gathering of many of the local church Sunday Schools in 1938, the parade being led by the banner of the Poole Salvation Army. In recent years, the Friends of Poole Park have instituted an August Bank Holiday Fest to raise funds for improvements to the park.

Other organisations have been allowed fundraising events in the park during the summer, including an annual event for the Mayor's charity. All make sure to include plenty of activities to attract children.

A Civil Defence exercise held in the 1950s behind the HQ hut at the back of the Municipal Buildings features in the old view. Post Second World War, Britain was soon in fear of another outbreak of hostilities when the Communist-ruled USSR developed nuclear warhead capability and had a frosty relationship with Western Europe. The British government organised a Civil Defence Force to deal with conditions after a nuclear bomb attack. This picture shows volunteers from the local Women's Volunteer Service demonstrating their culinary skills in an emergency field kitchen. The large building in the background is the Sloop Hotel.

After Civil Defence was disbanded, the site became a staff car park, nicknamed 'St Andrews'' by staff working for one of the authors, who was Town Clerk and CEO at the time the Municipal Buildings were extended and renamed as the Civic Centre.

Commercial Road leads from the Civic Centre to the shopping centre at Parkstone. The Lloyds Bank branch was built in 1932 to meet the need for a 'resident banker' conveniently close to the brand new Municipal Buildings. The adjoining petrol station (now a car showroom) was also a convenience until the 1960s when safety legislation prevented the service of fuel from swing pumps over the highway.

And what would complete the needs of a new office? Well, a public house, of course, but fortunately one already existed in the Sloop, built in the 1820s before the railway arrived in Poole and when the sea came up to the original shoreline in what is now Poole Park. It was reportedly named after the wrecks of old sloops to be found on that shore.

After a frivolous and brief name change to the Conjurer's Half Crown, the pub has thankfully reverted to its original name.

The then vicar of St Peter's Church, Canon Dugmore, led many campaigns for Parkstone. One of these led, in 1899, to the building, by W.A. Cross & Sons of Commercial Road, to an Area Municipal Office at the junction of Britannia and Salterns Roads. The clock is nowadays inoperative, due to safety rules condemning the access to wind it up! The building housed a long awaited horse-drawn fire appliance, with stables. Apart from the offices there was a committee room, also used as a reading room, which became Parkstone's library in 1927. On the front right of the old picture is T. Moorshead, a florist's, fruiterer's and greengrocer's shop since 1888. When this shop was demolished, the Southern Electricity offices and showroom were erected and are now the print works of Minuteman. On the front left of the picture, Taylor's was a family butcher that became a fish and chip shop which was later demolished and is now incorporated in a highway verge.

Station Road, Parkstone

Lower Parkstone has been a thriving village for over 150 years, with its own green, pubs and shops, supplying most of the needs of the local residents. Little has changed over the years apart from the names over the shops. At the time of the early photograph, around 1915, taken at the junction of Station Road and Commercial Road, Leverett & Frye, the largest grocer in the 'village' also had premises in Bournemouth Square. Hunts was a private library, and other shops in the road included a chemist (still there under different ownership). Parkstone Post Office was originally next door to Hunts. It later moved to its present site in Bournemouth Road and by 1935, the old Post Office was used as the Christian Science Reading Room. Also in Station Road there was a branch of J.A. Hawkes & Sons, the well-known local shoe supplier. Local ironmongers, Bacon and Curtis, occupied the shop that is now the premises of an Indian takeaway and Frost & Co. estate agents.

Parkstone Green (as the park was originally known) was laid out by the Council in the late 1880s, at the same time as Poole Park, at a cost of £560. It included an elegant fountain (not the present concrete monstrosity that is due to be replaced) in an area once known as Three Acres Field. Providing a new park was another of Canon Ernest Dugmore's campaigns for more recognition and better facilities for Lower Parkstone.

4

LILLIPUT TO COUNTY GATES

North Haven Point, *c.* 1920.

The Beehive Hotel, with its large rear garden, was a landmark for visitors from far and wide who were travelling to and from the beaches. It was also greatly appreciated by residents from the local area as there were no competing public houses in the vicinity. The loss of this 'local' for a development of retirement apartments was bitterly opposed by many, but the large site was an obvious target for developers, demonstrating the way land values have escalated over recent years.

In the old photograph, the thatched houses and the village school on the right in Sandbanks Road have given way to bungalows and a petrol filling station, which incorporates a Somerfield convenience store.

Boats have been built and repaired in Poole Harbour for over 3,000 years. The earliest known, a late Iron Age log boat discovered in 1964, has now been conserved and is a prized exhibit displayed in Poole Museum. The tradition of boat building for fishing and the transatlantic trade with Newfoundland was maintained from the Middle Ages onwards around the Quay and Hamworhy area.

When leisure boating became popular in the late nineteenth and early twentieth centuries, smaller yacht building and repair yards were established.

Walton Yacht and Launch Works was one of four boat builders listed in Poole in 1936. The approach to the yard was an inlet next to then Harbour Club at Salterns, built for her son's employment by the landlady of the Sea View Hotel. Pizeys Pier (formerly Knight's), which was demolished in the late 1990s, is in the background. Today, with the popularity of boating, the club has become the Salterns Hotel and a marina accommodating many luxury craft.

The old photograph is from the end of the Second World War and the days when BOAC operated flying boats all over the Empire from Salterns in Poole Harbour. Note the sign on the right; Poole was the birthplace of BOAC and for eight years, the harbour provided Britain's only international civil airport. After the war the premises became a boat sales showroom, now redeveloped as flats. Behind the sign lies an off-licence, kept in his latter days by the famous music hall artist, Fred Karno, whose mistress, from Parkstone, became his second wife.

Lilliput shops were the height of modernity in the 1930s and little has changed architecturally in the modern view. The pharmacy remained a chemists shop until very recently and the off-licence is still an off-licence. However the arrival of a fish and chip shop and a branch of Tesco Express have somewhat altered the genteel tone of former years.

Flag Farm was one of the few buildings on old maps of Poole lying alongside the dusty unmade track between Parkstone and North Haven (Sandbanks Ferry) and dates back to at least the eighteenth century. It is said to have links with Isaac Gulliver, a notorious smuggler who reputedly reformed his ways when he married.

Sewage used to be conducted out to sea through cast-iron pipes. A seawall constructed over the sewer survives today, surmounted by splendid dolphin lampposts. However, the sewage is now pumped in the opposite direction to an inland treatment works. Poole was the first local town to eliminate this health risk.

On a breezy day, the shallow Whitley Lake is a popular spot for wind and kite surfing. When the prevailing gales blow from the south-west, this stretch of road can become submerged from the spray over the wall and the stream overflowing from Parkstone Golf Course through Luscombe Valley (now a local nature reserve).

Sandbanks peninsula is now one of the most expensive residential areas in the world, with some houses in the area costing many millions of pounds. When this part of Poole was originally developed, the land cost just a few pounds an acre and many of the more prosperous had summer retreats built as their holiday getaways. Very few main homes were built. Sandy Hollow, now Grasmere Road (pictured) was a sandy track in this sparsely developed area in the 1920s, near to 'Landmark' on High Horse Manger, the highest point. Sandbanks very quickly became a sought after area and the original older properties on the sea front or main Panorama Road were demolished to make way for flats and larger houses. Because of the type of detached housing in Grasmere Road, it retains a more open atmosphere than the many apartment blocks in other roads on the Sandbanks peninsula.

The Haven Hotel, alongside Sandbanks Ferry, commands magnificent views across Poole Bay and into the narrow entrance to Poole Harbour. An aerial at the Haven was used by Marconi to broadcast messages, initially to his ship in Poole Bay, the *Ellettra*, and ultimately across the Channel to France.

Guests travelling to the hotel were met from Bournemouth West Railway Station on a motor bus run by the proprietor, Eugene Poulain.

Alongside the hotel and a modern block of flats, the slipway for the ferry to and from Shell Bay can be seen in the modern view. This route, via Studland to Swanage, started in 1926, and saves motorists a long detour by road. The shoreline of Poole Harbour, with all its inlets, measures over 100 miles, and it is the largest natural harbour in Europe and one of the largest in the world.

View from the Pavilion, Sandbanks.

During the Depression in 1928, building the pavilion at Sandbanks was a bold (but controversial, even then) move by the Council to capture a share of the holiday tourist market. The distinctive and stylistic building, opened by Alderman Hunt, then Mayor, was designed in-house by the Borough Engineer, Ernest Goodacre, and has stood the test of time.

Originally the roof was a flat viewing platform, but this has now been tiled in traditional fashion because of maintenance problems. Its single-storey (limited by an Act of Parliament) colonnaded face to the road is matched by a curving 'suntrap' facing the sea, but externally the landscape has been altered over the years. A paddling pool and even a 'witches' ball' in the old days have become merely tarmac and an ornamental flowerbed. To improve the first impressions to the public of the town's (maybe the country's?) leading beach in this much-hyped area, palm trees have been planted and the putting green diminished to install more juvenile amusements.

In post-war days, early morning bathers and dog walkers at Sandbanks would have encountered the unusual sight of racehorses training on the beach! Mrs Louie Dingwall, the first woman trainer to be recognized by the Jockey Club, had her stables in Panorama Road nearby. The horses she trained included one named Poole Park, owned by Freddy Rowe, a wealthy local builder and former Mayor and Alderman of the Borough. Before she married, Miss Foott, as she then was, owned, ran and used to drive buses on a route still known today as the Rossmore Flyer, serving Upper Parkstone's side roads.

In 2008 horses were once again commmanding attention on the beach when the Council allowed a pilot prestigious world beach polo event, a first for the UK, having previously been held in Dubai, attracting many free-spending socialites to the resort. The public were allowed a free view from a bespoke sandbank on the seaward side. Its success led to the event being booked for this location each July for the next five years.

In the 1920s Shore Road at Sandbanks very quickly became popular with visitors and locals. Wooden beach huts were soon erected to provide privacy and storage facilities for those who were lucky enough to own one. These huts had no uniformity and because of the high winds and salt air, unless there was good, regular maintenance, the wooden huts soon disintegrated. To improve the look of the area and to halt the shore erosion, the Council cleared the old huts and built the promenade and erected the stronger brick and concrete huts. At the same time, private enterprise built a beach café and a hotel nearby, as well as private dwellings in the (still) privately maintained Chaddesley Wood Road. Further along the beach in the old postcard view, the remains of Simpson's Folly (an early concrete house foolishly built on sand) are visible.

Scott & Scott were well-established ironmongers on the north side of the Haven shopping parade (at No. 23), run by a Mr Ernie Eldridge in the 1930s, and supplying everyday needs of the local village. Such shops have long disappeared, replaced by a clutch of eating establishments, estate agents and banks. Indeed, one of the former 'big five' banks was bold enough to be the first in the country to say that while it would provide a bank ATM here for all to make withdrawals, it would only provide their other bank services for clients holding deposits of at least £50,000 at the branch. Other clients with smaller accounts would have to use their other branches!

The Esplanade, Canford Cliffs

The Esplanade, Canford Cliffs, was built with fine mansions overlooking Canford Cliffs Chine and Poole Bay, near the Canford Cliffs Hotel, with a Martello-type tower in the grounds. This hotel was destroyed by an incendiary bomb in 1941 and the former chauffeurs' quarters became a public house that gained a reputation as a haunt for the many showbiz personalities. Rebuilt, it is now known as the 'Nightjar'.

Some of the mansions in the Esplanade were taken over by hotels, such as the 'well appointed' thirty-bedroom Riviera, with 'First class chefs and a fine cellar.' As the modern view shows, it has now been demolished and redeveloped as a block of luxury flats.

As a popular spot to begin exploration of the chines and beaches of Poole, the adjoining roads have been heavily regulated by yellow lines; indeed, the zealous pursuit of revenue by a 'hit squad' posse of traffic wardens nearly prevented the cameraman's car being stopped long enough to obtain this view!

THE ZIG-ZAG, BRANKSOME.

Lying between Canford Cliffs Chine and Branksome Chine, the 1930s saw the area's attraction to tourists enhanced by generous landscaping. A thatched chalet, nestling among the native pine trees, provided a welcoming resting place for weary walkers. Their view was over Poole Bay and the wide sweep of natural landscape before the promenades shown were constructed. Visitors can still make a descent to the beach down a zigzag path and steps. The clifftop has recently been cleared of invasive rhododendron and the clifftop footpath has been paved and decorated by local schoolchildren. The chalet still offers seating, but definitely not sleeping (or courting) facilities!

In the eighteenth and nineteenth centuries, the isolated cove of Branksome Chine was a favourite haunt of the local smuggling gangs and the natural landscape had not changed in 1905, as shown in the first photograph, when the main users of the beach were a few local fishermen. The development of the early 1930s to encourage tourism saw the stylish art deco solarium (now known as the upmarket Branksome Beach restaurant) built to boost the now-feared 'benefits' of ultra violet light and the sun's rays. A promenade was erected as protection for the crumbling cliffs. Early 1930s wooden beach huts were replaced by the concrete structures in the 1960s.

This previously unpublished picture of Branksome Chine car park shows the ramshackle facilities available to beach visitors in 1927. The restaurant was a pre-First World War thatched building with an adjacent small marquee serving as the café. Two children seem to be rinsing their swimming costumes in a wooden tub and an old oil drum is being used as a litter bin. Two bicycles, the popular mode of transport, are leant against the wooden buildings on the right. In the 1930s, with the growth of motoring and tourism, the Council cleared the site of the outdated buildings and developed facilities for visitors, including toilets and changing cubicles and an extended car park. These have changed very little over the last seventy-five years.

Branksome Chine

Looking east from Branksome Chine in around 1910 towards Bournemouth, the few beach goers are probably a family enjoying a day's outing. Modesty in dress was the norm of the period, with the young ladies tucking up their long skirts to go for a paddle in the shallow water at low tide. Older members of the family resting on deck chairs by the fishing boats on the shore are fully dressed from top to toe and sensibly shading themselves under umbrellas. Nearly everybody in the picture is wearing a hat as protection from the sun. A few wooden beach huts are at the bottom of the cliffs as a sign of the growing popularity of the area. In the background of the original picture, the Highcliff Hotel on the Bournemouth West Cliff can just be seen. The modern view shows the apartments at the clifftop that replaced the world-renowned Branksome Tower Hotel. It was Poole's only five star hotel.

A favourite walk for many generations has been through Branksome Woods. Starting at Penn Hill corner and finishing at Branksome Chine, the woods are particularly attractive when the rhododendron bushes are in bloom. When the facilities at the shore of Branksome Chine were built in 1932, the stream through the woods was laid out in the profile of the Solent coast, with the Isle of Wight in the middle of the then fast flowing water. This was much enjoyed by local children sailing their toy yachts. The flow of the stream is now reduced as road drainage from housing developments has piped off the amount of water reaching the stream. The crumbling path along the stream needs remedial work and the stream bed, now clogged with leaves and debris, needs constant clearing.

The Avenue is a broad boulevard, lined with trees and bushes leading from County Gates. It was originally a private carriageway for the Branksome Tower Hotel and its walled estate, but it is now better known as the route to Branksome Beach and car park. Cerne Abbas was one of the most imposing private mansions with extensive grounds that lined the road, and described by Pevsner as 'a Wagnerian fantasy in bright red brick Gothic with a high chateau-roofed tower'. It was built for the Packe family who owned the estate. One of the most famous occupants was J.J. Allen, who owned the Bournemouth department store of that name. Latterly it was a convalescent home. Just before it could be listed, in 1977, it was demolished for the current estate of more modest, but still expensive, mews-style town houses.

5

BRANKSOME, UPPER PARKSTONE AND NEWTOWN

Sea View Road.

The showrooms of F. English Ltd, Poole Road, Branksome, built in 1958, with a garage workshop and petrol filling facilities, broke the Branksome Park strict building conventions and was bitterly opposed by the local residents. F. English Ltd, owned by Col. Ronnie Hoare, was the local agent for Ford's and when the company moved in the late 1980s to a newly-built facility at Tower Park, the premises were used briefly as an indoor market, with a second-hand car dealer on the outside car park. Tesco's purchased the site in the early 1990s and submitted plans for a supermarket that was also unsuccessfully opposed by the local residents. After the opening of Tesco's in 1993, the filling station continued for several years as an independent business until Tesco's eventually took it over.

The Woodman public house in Poole Road was built in the 1850s at Branksome. It was a convenient stopping place on the dusty main road to Christchurch. When Bournemouth developed westwards, it was the nearest hostelry for the western end of the town. In 1968 the building was demolished and redeveloped as a then fashionable ten pin bowling alley, with a replacement Woodman public house next door.

With the opening of the through railway line to Bournemouth in 1872, it is surprising that the building of Branksome Station (with the strap line 'for eastern Poole') took until 1893, as this was a rapidly growing area. To provide for religious needs, the Wesleyans built a church near the station. With a fall in congregations, it became surplus to requirements and closed in the 1980s. The site was redeveloped as flats. On an adjoining former boys' club, the Jehovah Witness Hall was then self-built by the combined labours of the members of the congregation.

The Pineland Laundry at the junction of Alder Road with Ashley Road, next to the Bourne Valley Pottery, was owned by the Newton family. It provided two classes of laundry – the Pineland, for the many hotels and commercial businesses in the area, and the Popular, where the public could take and collect their domestic items from a green door in Alder Road.

The premises were bombed in 1941 and the Collar Room was destroyed. By conveying items to Boscombe in wicker baskets, the service was able to continue until repairs were completed.

The site is now embodied in the garden section of the Homebase store at Branksome Commercial Centre.

In the heyday of safe cycling, when cars were an expensive luxury rather than an everyday necessity, depots sold, hired, and repaired bikes, as well as selling spares and were the equivalent of today's garages. Bushby's Victory Cycle Depot at No. 88 Bournemouth Road was well placed to serve a wide public. The photograph shows that his trade was expanding to meet a new demand for motorbikes. At this time there was a frequent tram service between County Gates and Poole passing his door, well used by people with jobs in other parts of the Poole and Bournemouth conurbation.

The modern use of the premises is by a ventilation and air conditioning supplier and a clothes shop.

In 1912, Ashley Road, Branksome, was a busy suburb of Poole and until 1905 had been independent of the town as a separate urban district, evidenced by its offices in Library Road, now known as Bob Hann House. The tram service, driven by an overhead power supply suspended from ornate poles, ran between Poole, Upper Parkstone and County Gates. It started in 1901 and ran until Hants & Dorset Motor Services Ltd introduced a substitute bus service in June 1935. The original tram fare from Albert Road to County Gates was 1*d*, with 3*d* the fare to Poole Railway Station at Towngate Street.

Until the arrival of supermarkets in the late 1950s, many of the shops were independent traders for everyday commodities.

Willis Bros were a Broadstone and Moordown-based builders' suppliers serving the conurbation who took on a block of five shops in Ashley Road in 1928, when they expanded into the tiling business. Designing and building tiled fireplaces with wooden mantelpieces became one of their most successful lines. In one exceptional week in 1937, they produced 167 fireplaces in seven days by working two shifts, day and night. In 1939 they produced a record 3,700 fireplaces – fixing sufficient tiles to make a footpath 1yd wide from Poole Quay to Bournemouth Pier! Some of these fireplaces remain in local houses built in the 1930s. The shops are now mainly occupied by a variety of motor trade and accessory suppliers and a fast food outlet.

In the Poole estate of Blandford brewers Hall & Woodhouse were a number of off-licensed premises, as well as its many public houses. This one in Ashley Road at the junction with Layton Road was photographed in 1927. The pillar outside is not a post box, but a control box for the tram service that conveniently passed the door. The advert boards show the forthcoming programmes for the Grand at Westbourne and the Victory Palace Cinema further along Ashley Road.

By the 1960s the premises became the Edelweiss Restaurant. The small forecourt would then be full of customers' cars until late in the evening. The restaurant was later converted to a very successful ladies' beauty business, known as Bodycare, established by a young lady who was assisted by a grant from the Prince's Trust (mentored by one of the authors of this book).

Between 1873 and 1885 Heatherlands School, between Cromwell and Beaconsfield Roads, was a British School. It was then enlarged and taken over by the Council as a girls' and infants' school. One of the teachers became the wife of the Poole Librarian and author of local books, Bernard Short, and was forced to resign because married ladies were not then allowed. She fought the case and won a short-lived victory, but on appeal the Council won the day. She resumed teaching, but it was in private schools in the Borough.

The site of Heatherlands School has now been redeveloped for private housing.

Field's Garage and the workshops behind in Ashley Road, photographed around 1930, not only sold and serviced popular British makes of cars, but supplied Shell petrol from a swing arm pump while the motorists waited at the kerbside. The local Dorset registration numbers commenced 'PR'. The range of shops retain their original domestic features. The forecourts (or front gardens originally) today form a wide pavement in front of one of the many estate agents that have invaded this and many other shopping parades. The former workshops are not wasted, but after many other uses, are currently used as a carpet warehouse. The Midland Bank (now HSBC) is one of the few premises in this parade to retain its original use.

ASHLEY ROAD LOOKING EAST, PARKSTONE.   H. 1438.

These photographs illustrate the changes in Ashley Road (looking east from the Richmond Road, formerly Sandy Lane, junction) between 1945 and the present day.

Poole & Parkstone Co-operative Society's department store on the left is now largely the Parkstone, a public house. The prominent white building beyond it was the Regal Cinema. On its site a Boots Chemists, a betting office and an Iceland store now trade. Further in the distance, Co-op retains a food supermarket built on the site of a former Butler's furnishing store. Sadly, Woolworths ceased trading as this book was being written and it has been occupied by an 89p discount shop.

On the right, note how former tram poles have been converted to streetlights and how a Belisha beacon then coped with pedestrians crossing, though without the zebra markings at that date. With increased numbers of cars, a traffic light system, with a pedestrian phase, together with safety barriers has been installed.

The Retreat, Ashley Road, Upper Parkstone, a Strong's of Romsey (later Whitbread's) public house offering hotel accomodation, was a prominent building from the 1880s and in its heyday, because of the easy access to Poole and Bournemouth, a favourite place for commercial travellers to stay whilst working in the area. The pub was closed in the early 1980s and the site was developed by Safeways as a supermarket with a two-level underground car park. After Morrison's purchased Safeways, the shop was surplus to their requirements. Waitrose seized the opportunity to move to the premises in 2006, closing their smaller Westbourne shop, much to the annoyance to some of their Westbourne customers. To the right of the Retreat, partly visible, was a tram depot and booking office. The booking office survived the redevelopment of the Retreat, but has closed in recent years.

Stainers shoe shop has been known to generations as a suppliers and shoe repair shop. But its origins are shown here, in Sea View Road, where the business was founded by David Skinner's grandfather, like many other businesses, in his home. Note in this 1910 photograph the workshop to the left of the semi-detached house.

The present business premises are in Ringwood Road and bear the scar of a Second World War bombing raid, from which the family were lucky to escape alive.

Sea View Rd & Poole Rd, Newtown.

What has changed in these views of the junction of Sea View Road and Ringwood Road over the years? The most prominent building is the former Post Office at the junction. The roads themselves were sandy and covered with gravel. Telephone poles are apparent, but no street lights. Who would walk in the middle of the thoroughfare today without fear of being killed or injured?

Today, traffic lights are needed to regulate the traffic flows and this is one of the busiest road junctions in the borough.

The painting shows a thriving Kinson Pottery in Ringwood Road. At the time it was producing a wide variety of glazed stoneware pipes, bricks and other products from the local clay pits. The owner of the pottery from 1908 was Herbert S. Carter, grandson of Jesse Carter, the founder of Poole Pottery. Apart from his business, Herbert Carter OBE was an author and was prominent in civic affairs, having been Mayor five times and a Freeman. Dedicated to Poole and its people and the harbour he loved, a secondary school in Hamworthy was named after him to recognise his particular contribution to Poole's education system. His home at the Hermitage, Parkstone Heights, overlooked the works. The pottery closed in 1970 and the site, including some of the original buildings, is now a thriving industrial trading estate.

Opposite Kinson Pottery and originally surrounded by clay workings, there has been a pub-cum-hotel on this site since the nineteenth century, used mainly for refreshment by the local manual workers. The beer came from Poole's Dolphin Brewery.

Early in the twentieth century, the premises were rebuilt as we see them today. It became a Strong's of Romsey (later Whitbread) house and now serves both an industrial estate and homes built on former clay pits in the Haymoor and Foxholes area.

The Regent filling station (Harbour Hill Garage) displays the then popular method of discounting and obtaining loyalty by offering Green Shield stamps. These premises are now a block of flats.

The Ryvita Crispbread Bakery, Old Wareham Road, is part of the Associated British Foods conglomerate. The company moved its production of crispbread from Birmingham to Poole in 1949, as it was close to a port. The production of Ryvita expanded rapidly with the growth of the health food market. The company takes the name of Poole around the globe. In recent years, new varieties of the product have been introduced and new technologies have been adopted to retain its dominant position in the market.

   The front of the factory was remodelled in the early 1970s to accommodate the main offices. In 2008 the company merged with Jordans Health Bars, with ABF as the majority shareholder, and moved its joint head office to Bedfordshire, retaining the production of crispbread in Poole. One of the authors of this book was an employee of the firm for twenty-nine years.

6

LONGFLEET TO NORTHERN POOLE

Oakdale from the air, 1938.

This post-war panorama of Longfleet shows Parkstone and Longfleet Roads converging. The twin chimneys of the Generating Station at Hamworthy, in the background, dominated views from miles around. This part of Poole arose as an overspill suburb of the crowded Old Town from about 1830 onwards and the streets are lined with Victorian villas. Many of these are now in commercial use or provide accommodation for hospital staff.

The landmark building in the modern view housed the HQ of what was then the Dominion, Colonial and Overseas branch of Barclays Bank, relocated from the City of London. It processed all the bank's travellers' cheques and required modern electronic links. Such is the speed of change in technology that a further review of its function has led the bank to give notice that it requires less staff and space, leaving part of the premises to be leased to new occupants. The symbolic eagle that dominated the building has now been dismantled.

Lady Cornelia Wimborne, a great benefactor of Poole, provided a hospital in West Street and when this proved too small, transferred it to the Hermitage in Weston's Lane, and later still to Sir Peter Thompson's former house in Market Street. Her offer to the Council to donate a cottage hospital to celebrate Queen Victoria's Golden Jubilee was rejected in favour of a new library, donated by Mr J.J. Norton, timber merchant and well-known leader of the teetotal movement.

By 1906 it was obvious that larger facilities were needed and Lord Wimborne then gave two and a half acres next to Longfleet Church for a new hospital, named after his wife, Cornelia. It opened in 1907. With numerous expansions, these buildings survived until 1962, when the hospital was redeveloped and considerably enlarged. The new Poole General Hospital was officially opened by the Queen in July 1969. Poole Hospital became a NHS Foundation Trust in October 2007.

From a once busy pre-war goods yard, pictured here, railways goods traffic has declined locally to the point where barely a siding is needed. In the background were private allotments, now sacrificed for additional land for Henry Harbin School. Before the Second World War, the railway line had a branch running down West Quay Road to the Quay, where goods were transferred into wagons as well as lorries. The closure of the Somerset and Dorset line to Bath under the Beeching cuts in the 1960s also led to the decline of goods traffic. Poole Station itself has been rebuilt from the original gas-lit building twice since the 1960s, now being little better than a Portakabin, but there are plans for a third version to form a full town traffic interchange, including buses and coaches, absorbing the old goods yard land.

Sterte Esplanade, as it was in 1936, enjoyed a water frontage giving direct access for boat owners to Holes Bay. A historic area, Sterte has yielded a hoard of Roman coins. Being at the edge of shallow water, at low tide the area was distinctly malodorous! For many years a cannon, reputedly captured in the Crimean War, was prominently displayed. The cannon was later moved to Poole Park where it remained until the Second World War, when it was taken for scrap metal for the war effort. Post-war, the medium-rise flats in the modern view were constructed by the Council. After infilling, Holes Bay Road was constructed in the late 1980s to provide a much-needed fast route out of town, but at the price of taking away the water frontages, leaving an area of open space. Further development in this area is under construction, maintaining the pleasant outlook.

Poole Town Football Club has gone full circle (it was founded in 1890) in its search for a permanent home. From playing at Tatnam at the turn of the twentieth century, they played at various grounds; in Breakheart Lane (now known as Fernside Road) and Stokes Field at Oakdale, before moving to the newly built Poole Stadium in Wimborne Road in the early 1930s. In 1994 the club were ejected from the stadium, so that greyhound racing and Poole Pirates speedway could have exclusive use. After sharing grounds with Hamworthy United and Holt United for short periods and playing at Haskells Recreation Ground in Newtown, an agreement was reached for them to share a pitch with the new Oakdale South Road Middle School at Tatnam.

Controversially, the club submitted a plan in 2008 to build an enclosed pitch at Branksome Recreation Ground. This would enable them to meet FA requirements to move up the non-league pyramid and provide improvements to the pavilion and public facilities already there. At the time of going to press, the outcome is uncertain.

The earlier photograph shows action at Poole Stadium and the recent photograph was taken at the shared Tatnam Playing Fields.

In both of these views of Tatnam Road at the junction with Sterte Road, Tatnam Farmhouse appears in the background. The farmhouse has been on the site for well over 150 years and has been used for many purposes, including a cattery. The outer farm buildings, including the barns and cottages for the farm employees, have been demolished. Part of the farm ground has been incorporated into the public recreation ground part which is now shared between playing fields for Oakdale South Road Middle School and Poole Town FC (as described for the previous photograph)

It was at this spot, from manorial days, that the town's original source of water was drawn from a conduit or well. It was licensed to be improved by Henry VIII in 1542, and is now capped off under a property in Well Lane.

Fernside Garage (owned by A.H. Moorman), with its prominent fuel signs on the roof, was situated at No. 137 Fernside Road. A greengrocer and fruiterer, a hairdresser and a tobacconist occupied the adjoining shops. After the retirement of Mr Moorman, the block was rebuilt with a Total fuel station with a garage workshop attached. With the closure of the filling station, there was a further redevelopment of the site with a One Stop convenience store that has now become a Tesco Express.

Opposite the store shown in the previous photograph, at the junction with Pound Lane, shop customers can see an oak post marking the site of the original Longfleet Pound (one of three in the town) for stray cattle and horses, recalling the days when this area was farmland.

Dorchester (formerly Cemetery) and Ringwood Roads are two of the oldest routes in the local road network. At the junction of these roads, looking towards Newtown in around 1905, stand the younger members of the Frend family, who lived in the row of houses on the right. They could stand in the middle of the highway to have their picture taken without fear of any cars. Many of the houses were occupied by employees of the Kinson Pottery that was further along the road on the right. St Clement and St Barnabas Church, built in 1889, can just be seen in the background. The turning on the right, known locally as Bridle Path, is also of early date, being shown as a lane on early maps of Poole. It remained an unmade track to Parkstone Heights until the 1990s. The grocer's shop on the right was converted into a private residence in recent years.

The parish of St Mary's Longfleet (whose first Rectory was an old thatched house in what is now named Rectory Road) originally embraced Oakdale. With the rapid development of housing after the First World War, there was a need to establish a more local venue for the Anglican community to worship. In 1932 the first St George's Church (pictured) was built at the junction of Dorchester Road and Wimborne Road as a daughter church of St Mary's, replacing an old barn in Darby's Lane that had been used for some services. St George's was declared a parish in 1944. This first St George's Church was always regarded as a temporary church and with further development post-war, a decision was taken to build a larger church complex. The present St George's (pictured) in Darby's Lane was consecrated on 11 July 1960. The old church was then used as a temporary church hall, but is now the Oakdale branch of Poole's library service.

When several hundreds of acres of heathland at South Canford Heath were bought by
the Council in 1963 for town expansion, an access had to be created under the A35 (Old
Wareham Road – now known as Dorset Way). These pictures show the site of the underpass
under construction and the resulting roundabout built at the junction of Johnston Road and
Oakdale Road, along with the landscaping with heather and tree planting. The power lines in
the original view have been relocated.

At the left-hand side of the old picture can be seen the side of the 'Nissen hut-looking'
Oakdale/Poole Boys' Club. The club had originated as the Canford-Poole Boys' Club in the Old
Town and moved to Plainfield House in Waterloo Road before moving to Johnson Road. In
turn, this clubhouse was redeveloped for housing in the 1990s when a replacement club was
built on the by-then completed housing estate at South Canford Heath.

The South Canford Heath land was bought from Lord Wimborne to carry out a visionary expansion scheme to meet the pressure for housing and jobs and ensure the town's economy did not decline. Housing was built at affordable prices (the ones in view ranging from about £3,600 to £4,000 in 1963) by national developers and the infrastructure of roads, churches, shops and community buildings were timed to coincide with their completion.

The overall plan was controlled by the Council to ensure a mixture of houses and bungalows, with open plan front gardens and hidden television aerials (though the latter restriction had to be relaxed due to poor reception).

Young people achieved good results in local schools but were having to move elsewhere to find jobs that matched their skills. However, as new employers with a need for highly trained employees relocated into the town and created demand, many young people benefited from greater opportunities for them to stay.

Nags Head Farm in Waterloo Road was a dairy (latterly known as Bennett's Dairy), but it was originally built in 1819 as a beerhouse with its own brewhouse, then known as the Nags Head Inn, and also with stabling. This large, impressive building, between Fleetsbridge and Darby's Corner, was demolished for the widening of Waterloo Road.

A petrol filling station later built on the site was replaced in 2007 by an auto centre and a variety of eateries. At the northern end, farmland was sold for their playing fields when Parkstone Girls' Grammar School was relocated in 1962 from Ashley Cross. A small Plymouth Brethren chapel, now in use by the adjoining Girls' Grammar School, was built on the corner of Cabot Lane. It was erected by the Bennett family, who owned and ran the dairy.

S 10887   L. & S. W. RAILWAY STATION, BROADSTONE.

'Castleman's Corkscrew' was the original main line to London from Dorchester, via Brockenhurst and Southampton. To travel directly to London, Poole passengers had to join the train at Broadstone until Poole Station and the line via Bournemouth was opened in 1872.

The Pines Express from Manchester to the resorts of Poole and Bournemouth also ran through Broadstone Station by way of the Somerset & Dorset Railway (nicknamed the 'Slow and Dirty') as far as Bath. The S&D Railway served many rural villages, and was lost to passenger traffic in 1966 in the Beeching cuts. Its loss continues to be regretted.

Broadstone Leisure Centre and the adjoining car park now occupy the site of the station and track. To the right in the old picture stood the old Lavender Farm. The nearby Broadstone Railway Hotel has recently reopened to customers as the 'Goods Yard'.

VIEW OF NEW SHOWROOMS
ONE MINUTE FROM BROADSTONE STATION. 1908

William A. Willis started his builders' merchant business in 1904 in a shed in the garden of his house in Lower Golf Links Road but soon outgrew home-working and moved to premises he built in Moor Road near Broadstone station, shown in the old photograph. Its success led to branches in Moordown, Kinson and Ashley Road, Parkstone. His sons joined his business in 1934. Supplies were received by rail from a siding at Broadstone Station and delivered by their own fleet of lorries.

In 1943 the Moordown Head Office was damaged when a British bomber returning from France crashed there and in 1944 the Broadstone stores were devastated overnight by an incendiary bomb. The post-war years were a struggle under government building restrictions. W.A. Willis died in 1950. The business survived until the 1980s. The Broadstone shop premises now houses a café.

The firm and the family are commemorated by the naming of Willis Way, leading from Fleets Lane to Broadstone Way.

In former years a typical and likely business to find in a remote rural part of northern Poole was the wheelwright and carriage- and wagon-building works of H.A. Gane, in what was then in Kinson tithing. (This part of Kinson tithing, including Broadstone, Merley, Canford and Ashington, was incorporated in the Borough of Poole in 1933.) A wide range of carts and carriages was made on the site and wind power was used to drive the belt-driven machinery, as mains electricity had not yet reached the area. The exact location is now hard to trace, but bears resemblance to the farm at Moortown, pictured on a site that runs down to the River Stour.

Other titles published by The History Press

Poole

IAN ANDREWS & FRANK HENSON

This fascinating collection of over 200 photographs of Poole complements an earlier volume in this series compiled by the same authors. This completely new collection of images takes the reader once again on a nostalgic journey through Poole to look at things as they were, not so very long ago. Once familiar buildings, shops and firms can be seen again and Poole people are seen involved in all manner of work and play activities. There is an interesting feature about Poole Town Football Club and another about Poole lifeboat. Schools, hospitals, pubs, churches and carnivals all make an appearance.

978 0 7524 0785 2

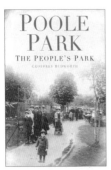

Poole Park: The People's Park

GEOFFREY BUDWORTH

From nannies pushing perambulators, children in sailor suits, and couples boating on the saltwater lake, *Poole Park: The People's Park* is a well illustrated and readable introduction to this Grade II listed heritage park and garden, and will appeal to the thousands of visitors who enjoy its facilities every year. An important feature of the book is a walking tour, which reveals the history of the park through its existing notable features.

978 0 7509 5092 3

Haunted Poole

JULIE HARWOOD

From heart-stopping accounts of apparitions, manifestations and related supernatural phenomena to first-hand encounters with ghouls and spirits, this collection of stories contains new and well-known spooky tales from in and around Poole. Drawing on historical and contemporary sources, *Haunted Poole* contains a chilling range of ghostly phenonema including the town's own tragic Romeo and Juliet tale, legendary Poole pirate Harry Paye and his ghostly galleon, the screams of Alice Beard and ghoulish beggars wandering the streets.

978 0 7524 4503 8

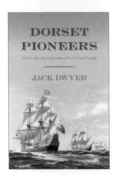

Dorset Pioneers

JACK DWYER

Professional writer Jack Dwyer reveals for the first time the intriguing link between a rural English county and the founders of seven US states, four Canadian provinces, a society doyen, an ambassador of the United States, a US Presidential candidate fundraiser and a Christchurch schoolma'am. This absorbing and beautifully written book traces the North American connection with Dorset characters such as Sir Walter Raleigh and the Tolpuddle Martyrs.

978 0 7524 5346 0

Visit our website and discover thousands of other History Press books.

www.thehistorypress.co.uk